LEAVES and TREES

TEXT BY ELAINE PASCOE

PHOTOGRAPHS BY DWIGHT KUHN

BLACKBIRCH PRESS, INC.

WOODBRIDGE, CONNECTICUT

Published by Blackbirch Press, Inc.
260 Amity Road
Woodbridge, CT 06525

To Hillary
–D.K.

©2001 by Blackbirch Press, Inc.
Text ©2001 by Elaine Pascoe
Photographs ©2001 by Dwight Kuhn (unless otherwise noted)
First Edition

Email: staff@blackbirch.com
Web site: www.blackbirch.com

Printed in the United States

10 9 8 7 6 5 4 3 2 1

Photo Credits: All photographs ©Dwight Kuhn, except page 24: ©Corel Corporation.

front cover: autumn leaves
back cover: oak tree flowers, acorns forming on an oak tree, acorn germinating, adult oak tree

Library of Congress Cataloging-in-Publication Data
Pascoe, Elaine.
Leaves and Trees / by Elaine Pascoe ; photographs by Dwight Kuhn.
    p. cm. — (Nature close-up)
   ISBN 1-56711-474-1 (hardcover : alk. paper)
   1. Leaves—Juvenile literature. 2. Leaves—Experiments—Juvenile literature. 3. Trees—Juvenile literature. 4. Trees—Experiments—Juvenile literature. 5. Botany projects—Juvenile literature. [1. Trees. 2. Trees—Experiments. 3. Leaves. 4. Leaves—Experiments. 5. Experiments.] I. Kuhn, Dwight, ill. II. Title.
QK649 .P37 2001   00-011915
581.4'8—dc21   CIP
                                                                               AC

Note on metric conversions: The metric conversions given in Chapters 2 and 3 of this book are not always exact equivalents of U.S. measures. Instead, they provide a workable quantity for each experiment in metric units. The abbreviations used are:

cm	centimeter	**kg**	kilogram
m	meter	**l**	liter
g	gram	**cc**	cubic centimeter

CONTENTS

1

The Plant Kings

A large oak tree is a magnificent sight. An oak may live for hundreds of years, growing until it towers 100 feet (30 m) above the ground. But the oak isn't the world's biggest or tallest tree. The gold medal for height goes to the California redwood, which grows three times as tall as the oak. One California redwood is 364 feet (111 m) tall! But the redwood isn't the biggest tree. The giant sequoia is stouter than the redwood and that makes it the biggest.

Decaying leaves and trees enrich the surrounding soil.

The California redwood and the giant sequoia—which also grows in California—are two amazing trees. Many other trees are amazing, too. Trees are the kings of the plant world. They play key roles in keeping the living world humming along. They provide homes for many kinds of animals. Their leaves provide food and help to provide oxygen to the atmosphere. Even dead trees and leaves help the Earth by enriching the soil as they decay. Without trees, our planet would be a very different place.

Many types of birds and animals make their homes in tree trunks and the surrounding branches.

6

TREE TRAITS

Trees grow almost everywhere, except in the driest and coldest places. Worldwide, there may be more than 50,000 different kinds, or species, of trees. Each one is well suited to the land and climate where it grows. Bristlecone pines thrive in poor, dry soil where other trees can't grow. Palms and other tropical trees need warmth and moisture. They can't survive cold winters. In the far north, spruces and fir trees survive temperatures that sometimes drop to -50 degrees F.

Right: **Some evergreen trees can survive in very cold, snowy climates.**
Below: **Red maples are commonly found throughout the eastern part of North America.**

The roots of some trees do not grow deep into the ground.

Fine root hairs allow a tree to draw water and minerals from the ground.

From forest giants to tiny saplings, trees have certain things in common. A tree is a woody plant with a trunk—a stout central column. The branches grow out from the trunk. The roots spread out from the base of the trunk into the ground. The roots are important in many ways. They anchor the tree so it won't topple over when the wind blows. Some trees have strong taproots that grow deep into the ground. Others have shallow roots that reach well beyond the spread of the tree's branches.

The most important job of roots is to help feed the tree. Delicate feeder roots are covered with fine root hairs that draw water and minerals from the soil. The water and minerals form a liquid called sap, which moves up through the trunk and out to the leaves.

The outer bark of a Scotch pine is made up of scaly plates.

LIVING LAYERS

A tree's trunk and branches are made up of several layers.

Bark: Bark keeps a tree from drying out and insulates it from heat and cold. Bark also keeps insects, bacteria, and fungi from damaging the tree. Trees have two layers of bark. The tough outer layer is dry and dead, but the inner layer is alive. As the tree grows, its outer bark cracks, flakes, and peels. More bark is always being added from the inside, so the tree is protected.

Each kind of tree has a different kind of bark. White birches have thin outer bark that peels up in curls. Oak bark is deeply wrinkled. Scotch pines are covered in scaly plates of bark.

The tree's inner bark has a special job. Food that is made in the leaves flows down through this layer to all parts of the tree—branches, trunk, and roots.

The thin outer layer of white birch bark peels and curls.

Cross section of an oak trunk

Heartwood   Annual Rings

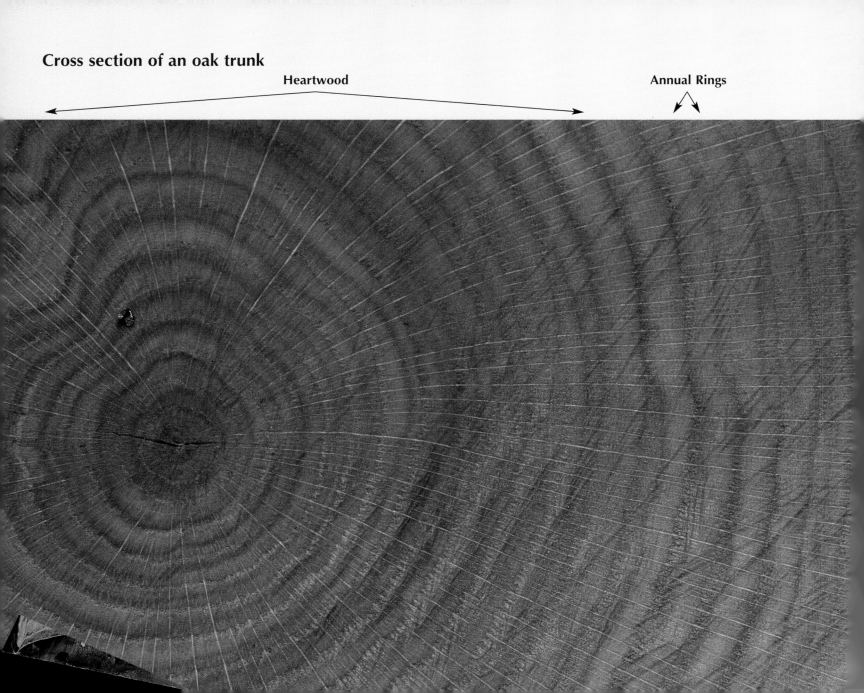

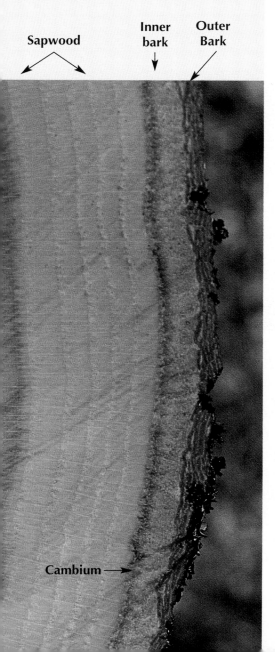

Sapwood Inner bark Outer Bark

Cambium

Cambium: Just under the bark is a thin layer called the cambium. It allows the trunk and branches to grow. Like all living things, trees are made up of tiny cells. Cells in the cambium divide, forming new cells that add to the thickness of the trunk and branches. New cells on the outer side of the layer develop into new bark. New cells on the inner side become new wood.

Sapwood: Under the cambium is a layer of living wood called sapwood. This layer carries sap from the roots to the leaves. Most of the cells in this layer line up in columns, and sap is pushed up the column as if it were a pipe. The sapwood layer is also the place where the tree stores food it may later need for growth or seed production.

Heartwood: New layers of sapwood form each year. As the tree ages, the innermost layers die. They form heartwood, the core of the tree. Heartwood helps make the trunk and branches strong. In old trees, the heartwood sometimes rots. Then the weakened tree may blow over in a storm.

When a tree is cut, you can estimate its age by counting the annual rings in a cross section of the trunk. The growth layers form the rings. Spring growth produces a band of light-colored wood. Summer and fall growth produces a narrower band of darker wood. Each ring of light and dark bands, together, shows a year's growth.

13

Many leaf species have interesting vein patterns.

LEAVES: FOOD FACTORIES

Leaves are solar-powered food factories. They use the energy from sunlight to make food for the tree. This process is called photosynthesis, from the Greek words for "light" and "putting together." The raw materials that leaves put together include water and minerals from the soil, and carbon dioxide gas from the air.

Here's how it works. Leaves contain a green pigment called chlorophyll. Chlorophyll draws energy from sunlight and turns it into a form of chemical energy. That chemical energy is used to turn the raw materials into a kind of sugar called glucose. Glucose gives the tree energy for growth and other needs. The tree uses it to make starch, cellulose (the main ingredient in wood), and even protein.

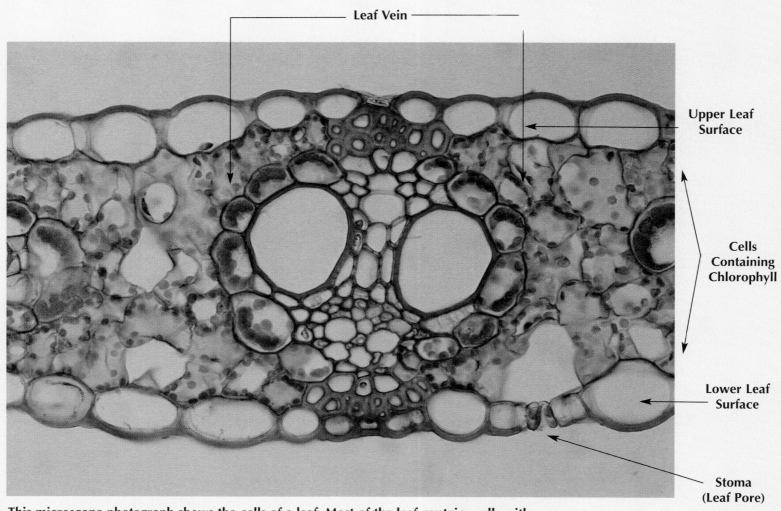

Leaf Vein

Upper Leaf
Surface

Cells
Containing
Chlorophyll

Lower Leaf
Surface

Stoma
(Leaf Pore)

This microscope photograph shows the cells of a leaf. Most of the leaf contains cells with
chlorophyll. The chlorophyll is stained blue-green in this photograph.

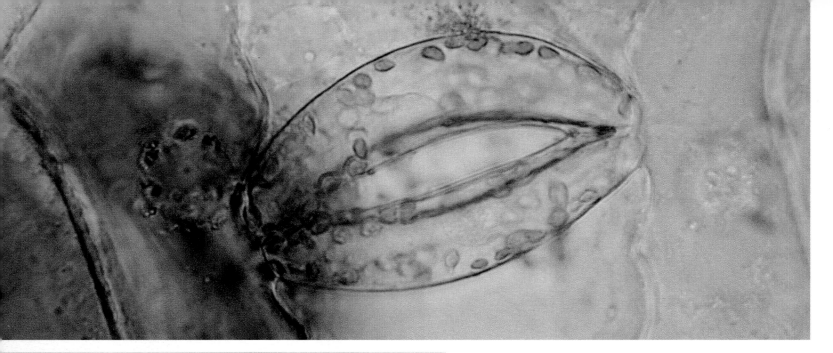

When a leaf's stoma is open (above), it can give off water in the form of vapor. A closed stoma (left) cannot give off water.

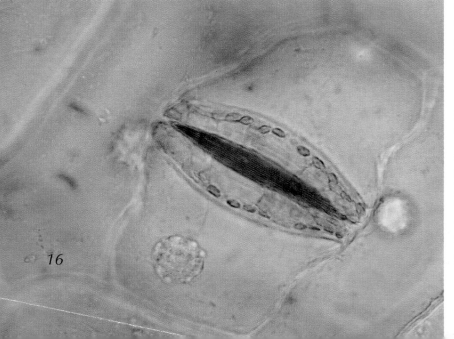

16

Water and oxygen are left over from the food-making process of photosynthesis. They're released into the air, mostly through countless tiny pores (called stomata) in the leaves. Although you can't see the water because it is in the form of vapor, trees do give off a lot of it. A large-sized oak tree may have up to 700,000 leaves and release 150 gallons (568 l) of water a day!

Light is very important to a tree, and a tree's leaves are arranged to catch it. They form a canopy over and around the trunk. Leaf arrangements vary, however, depending on the type of tree. For example, maple leaves grow in pairs. Birch leaves sprout from the branch in a staggered, alternating pattern.

Every kind of tree has a different kind of leaf. Leaf shapes, growth patterns, veins, and other features help people tell one type of tree from another. The box on page 21 has examples of several leaf types.

An evergreen is a type of tree that holds its leaves all year. Narrow-leaf evergreens, such as pines, have small leaves shaped like needles or scales. Broad-leaf evergreens include eucalyptus, laurel, holly, and many tropical trees.

An evergreen is a type of tree that holds most of its leaves all year.

In autumn, the leaves of deciduous trees turn brilliant colors because their green chlorophyll fades.

Deciduous trees shed their leaves each fall and grow new ones each year. As winter nears, these trees seal off the leaves' stems, so they're no longer supplied with sap. The chlorophyll, which makes the leaves green, fades. Many leaves then turn a brilliant color of yellow, orange, or red. The leaves have the pigments that make these colors all year, but the green chlorophyll masks them until fall.

The leaves of deciduous trees, as well as some pine needles, drop to the ground in autumn.

Eventually the weakened stems break away from the branches, and the leaves drop. They decay on the forest floor, enriching the soil. Trees such as maples, oaks, and elms stand leafless all winter. The buds that will form the next year's leaves are already on the branches. As spring nears, the trees' sap begins to flow and the buds swell. When warm weather returns, the buds open into new, bright green leaves.

Maple leaves emerge in the warm spring weather.

LEAVES OF MANY KINDS

You can recognize most kinds of trees by the shape of their leaves. Leaves may be simple (all one piece) or compound (made up of small leaflets). Here are some examples.

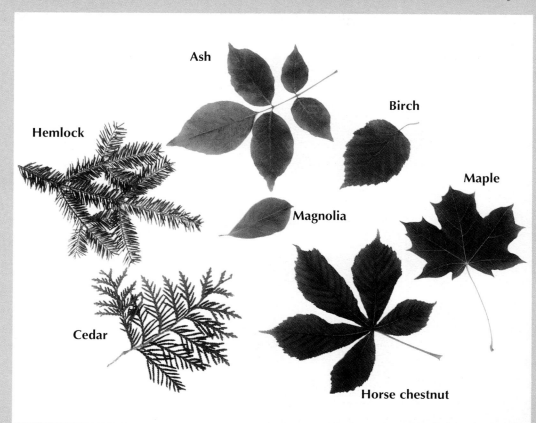

Birch: Simple leaf with toothed edges

Magnolia: Simple leaf with smooth edges

Maple: Simple leaf with lobed edges

Ash: Compound leaf, with pinnate leaflets (branching from a central stem)

Horse chestnut: Compound leaf with palmate leaflets (fanning from one point)

Hemlock: Evergreen needles

Cedar: Scale-like evergreen leaves

The very tiny flowers of oak trees (above)
need male pollen (left) to produce seeds.

SEEDS AND SAPLINGS

Many trees also burst into flowers
in spring. That's the first step in
creating seeds. All trees grow from
seeds, but many trees form seeds in
different ways.

Oaks, birches, and many other
trees have two kinds of flowers—
male and female. The male flowers
release pollen, and wind carries it
to the female flowers. The flowers
of other trees, including apples,
have both male and female parts.
Bees and other insects help carry
pollen from flower to flower. Once
flowers have been pollinated, seeds
begin to form.

There are as many kinds of seeds as there are kinds of trees. Some seeds are enclosed in fleshy fruits, such as apples and cherries. The seeds of some other trees, such as hickory and beech, are hard-shelled nuts. Pines, hemlocks, and most other narrow-leaf evergreens form seeds in cones. They are called conifers, which means "cone bearers."

For a new tree to sprout and grow, a seed must land in a place with water, light, and good soil. If a tree's seeds just fell straight down, the sprouts would never survive. The parent tree would block the sunlight and take most of the water. Instead, trees spread their seeds in various ways. Many seeds have papery wings that catch the breeze. The seeds of maple trees are covered by winged cases, called samaras.

Above: The seeds of hemlock trees form in cones.
Below: After pollination, acorns form on an oak tree branch.

23

WHAT A SAP!

Maple syrup and maple sugar are made from the sap of sugar maple trees. These trees are dormant and leafless in winter. But as spring nears, their sap begins to flow. People collect it by driving narrow tubes into the sapwood and attaching buckets to catch the sap that drips out. The sap is no thicker than water. To make syrup and sugar, it must be boiled down. It takes 30 gallons (113 l) of sap to make just one gallon (3.7 l) of syrup.

Tree sap also provides other products. Natural rubber is made from the sap of rubber trees, which are grown on plantations in tropical regions. Longleaf pine sap is used to make turpentine. Sap from tropical sapodilla trees provides chicle, an important ingredient in chewing gum.

Maple tree sap is collected in buckets (left) and boiled down to make syrup (right).

Animals also help spread seeds. A squirrel gathers acorns in the fall and buries them here and there. Some of the acorns will be winter food for the squirrel. But it won't eat all of them, and some acorns will sprout in the spring.

A sapling, or young tree, grows in all directions. The roots grow out and down, and the branches grow out and up. It takes many years for a tree to grow to full size. Growth rates vary with the kind of tree and the conditions where it grows. Some fast-growing trees can reach 40 feet (12 m) in 40 years. But other trees grow very slowly. A bristlecone pine may take 1,000 years to reach 40 feet (12 m).

The winged cases that contain maple tree seeds are called samaras.
Above left: Once an acorn germinates, the leaves, stem, and roots begin to grow.

25

TREES AND PEOPLE

People grow trees for many reasons. Some trees produce delicious fruits that are eaten as is, or turned into other food products. Wood from trees is burned as fuel, and used to make everything from pencils to houses to paper products. Many other products, including medicines, also come from trees.

The list of good things that trees do for people is long. Some of the most important things can't be seen. For example, trees help you breathe. Their leaves release large amounts of oxygen into the air. When you breathe, you take in oxygen and release carbon dioxide. Trees and other plants do the opposite. That helps keep the air breathable. Trees also help clean the air by trapping dust and pollutants.

Apples are just one kind of tree fruit people enjoy.

LEAF OR NOT?

Where are the leaves of a cactus? A cactus's leaves are its spines! A cactus stem stores water and makes food. Its sharp, needle-like leaves have another job. They protect the cactus from hungry desert animals.

Other leaves have special jobs, too. For example, most flowering plants have tiny specialized leaves called bracts at the base of each flower. But in some plants, the bracts develop until they look just like flower petals. The "flowers" of the dogwood tree are actually groups of large white bracts. The true flowers are small and hard to see. Many tropical plants, including poinsettias, also have petal-like bracts. These flashy leaves attract insects that pollinate the true flowers.

Forest preserves help protect healthy trees and the wildlife that depend on them.

28

Wind and water runoff cause erosion in areas where there are few tree roots in the soil.

Trees help drive the rain cycle, too. The water given off by tree leaves rises into the air. It forms clouds and falls again as rain. Trees then catch and filter rainwater. Their roots hold the soil and allow rain to sink into the ground, instead of running off. That reduces erosion, the wearing away of land by wind and water.

But people are cutting down forests at an alarming rate. Trees are cut for timber or cleared to make way for homes, shopping centers, farms, roads, and other kinds of development. Tropical rain forests are especially in danger. These forests are home to more different kinds of plants and animals than any other place on Earth.

Some people are taking steps to protect the forests. In some places, forest preserves have been set up. Saving trees is important because so many living things—including people—depend on them.

2

Collecting Leaves and Growing Trees

Trees are everywhere. Even in cities, you can find them in parks and squares and along many streets. You may pass dozens of trees a day and hardly give them a glance. If you take a closer look, you'll find that trees are easy and fun to investigate.

This chapter will help you get started. It will tell you how to collect and preserve leaves. You'll also find out how to grow a tree from seed, and how to plant a tree outside.

MAKE A LEAF COLLECTION

A leaf collection is a great way to begin learning about trees. Take leaves from different trees in your yard or a park near your home. Only take a couple of leaves from each tree. Try to choose the best ones you see—those with good color and no holes or insect damage.

The best way to save the leaves is to press them. Arrange single leaves between sheets of newspaper, blotting paper, or other absorbent paper. Put bricks or heavy books on top of the paper, and leave them there for several days. The leaves will dry flat.

A leaf collection will help you learn to identify different types of trees.

32

To preserve and press leaves, place them between sheets of newspaper, blotting paper, or other absorbent paper.

Use a tree guide from your school or public library to identify the leaves you've collected. Then mount your collection on poster board. Put a dab of rubber cement or other adhesive on the poster board where you want a leaf, and then gently press the leaf onto it. Label each leaf.

What You Need:

* Avocado
* Jar or other water container an inch or two wider than the seed
* Toothpicks
* Flower pot and potting soil

GROW AN AVOCADO TREE

You can grow a tree from an avocado you buy at the supermarket. The avocado is the fruit of the avocado tree, and its pit is the tree's seed.

What to Do:

1. Remove the seed from the fruit. Wash the seed, let it dry overnight, and remove the brown, papery outer coat.
2. Stick three toothpicks into the sides of the seed. Place the pit flat-side down in the water container, so that the toothpicks rest on the rim.
3. Fill the container with water until the bottom third of the pit is covered. Keep the container in dim light as roots grow. Check and add water as needed to keep the level the same. Change the water once a week.
4. When a stem starts to grow from the top of the pit, move the container to bright light. Continue to check and change the water.
5. When the stem is strong and the top of the pit splits apart, move the avocado seedling to a pot. Put in soil to cover the roots and the lower half of the pit. The stem and the top of the pit should be above the soil.
6. Water the plant to keep the soil damp but not soggy. Keep the pot in bright light. The seedling will eventually grow into an avocado tree. If you give it some fertilizer from time to time, it will grow faster.

GROW A PINEAPPLE TREE

You can grow a pineapple plant from the crown of a pineapple—the leafy part at the top.

What to Do:

What You Need:
* Fresh, ripe pineapple
* Large flower pot and potting soil

1. Ask an adult to cut the pineapple. Remove the crown first, leaving an inch or so of fruit attached to it.

2. Plant the crown in a flowerpot. Cover the fruit part completely with soil, so only the green leaves stick up.

3. Put the pot in a warm, sunny place. Water to keep the soil damp but not soggy. Roots will grow down from the base, and the crown will begin to grow into a new plant. Fertilizer will help it grow. When your pineapple plant gets bigger, you may want to move it to a larger pot.

Once the fruit of the crown has been planted, roots will begin to grow.

PLANT A TREE

Planting a tree is good for the environment, and it's a good family or group project. You can buy many kinds of trees at local nurseries. Small sizes are less costly and easiest to handle. Choose a site for your tree carefully. Make sure it will have enough light and room to grow.

Dig a hole for the roots. The hole should be larger than the root mass, so the roots will have room to spread and grow. It should be deep enough to cover the root mass, but not so deep that part of the tree's trunk is below ground. Pile the soil you dig from the hole onto a tarp. Mix some composted cow manure with the soil to enrich it.

Remove any burlap covering the roots. (If the tree is growing in a container, take it out.) Place the root mass in the hole and fill around the roots with the enriched soil.

After you dig a hole, carefully place the root mass in the ground and cover it with enriched soil.

When the hole is partly filled, tamp the soil down with your feet. Continue adding soil and tamping. Make sure the trunk is standing straight as you fill the hole.

Use loose soil to build a moat around the tree. Fill the area inside the moat with water, and let the water soak in. Then fill it again. Keep the tree well watered for the first year. But don't over-water, which will rot the roots. As a rule, water every three or four days during periods without rain.

Stake the tree to help the roots become established. Pound 2 or 3 sturdy stakes 12 to 18 inches (30 to 46 cm) into the soil, staying clear of the root mass. Loop strips of fabric around the tree and tie them to the stakes. This will help steady the tree on windy days, so the roots won't be disturbed as it sways in the wind. Remove the stakes in a year or so.

Left: **Stakes will help to keep the tree stable during windy days.** *Right:* **Water the tree well after planting.**

3

Investigating Trees and Leaves

Trees and their leaves are busy all the time—making food, circulating water, conditioning the air. But all this action is hidden from view because it's carried out by cells inside the plant. In the pages that follow, you'll find some experiments and activities that will help you learn more about the secret lives of trees and leaves.

HOW DO LEAVES USE WATER?

Water is used in the food-making process that takes place inside leaves. Do you think a branch with many leaves uses more water than a branch with fewer leaves? Answer based on what you know about trees. Then do this experiment to see if you are right.

What to Do:

1. Fill the bottles with water to within 2 inches (5 cm) of the top. Seal the tops with a golf-ball-sized glob of clay. Then carefully push a nail through the clay to make a narrow hole.
2. Clip the ends of the twigs to make a fresh cut. This will help them absorb water. Then put the cut ends through the clay holes, placing one twig in each bottle. Make sure the end of each twig is in the water. Then seal the clay around the twigs.
3. Place a sheet of plastic wrap over each twig and seal it with a clothespin or rubber band. Put the jars together in bright light (not direct sunlight). Check them in a few days.

Results: Compare the water levels in the bottles and the moisture in the plastic wrap. Which twig absorbed more water? Was all the water used in the leaves? If not, where did it go?

Conclusion: What do your results show about the needs of trees for water? Try this experiment again using twigs from different kinds of trees, but with the same number of leaves. Do different leaf species take in more water?

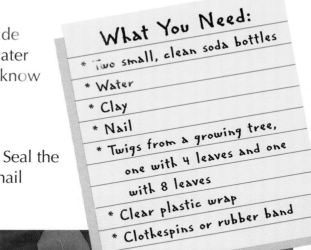

What You Need:
* Two small, clean soda bottles
* Water
* Clay
* Nail
* Twigs from a growing tree, one with 4 leaves and one with 8 leaves
* Clear plastic wrap
* Clothespins or rubber band

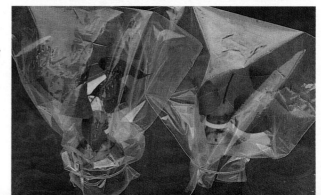

WHAT HAPPENS WHEN AIR CAN'T REACH LEAF SURFACES?

Leaves draw carbon dioxide from the air and release water and oxygen. This experiment will help you find out where most of that work is done—on the upper or lower side of the leaf. Before you begin, decide what you think the answer will be, based on what you know about leaves. Then check your answer against the results of the experiment.

What to Do:

1. Choose a leaf (or group of leaves) on one branch or section of the plant. Coat the top of the leaf (or leaves) with petroleum jelly. Cover the leaf with clear plastic, tied or fastened with a clothespin to the stem.
2. Choose a second leaf (or group) near the first. Coat the underside of the leaf (or leaves) with petroleum jelly. Cover with plastic, fastened as in step 1. If you think you may forget which leaf is which, label them.
3. Check the leaves every few days to see how much water has collected under the plastic. This is water given off by the leaves.

Results: Which leaf gave off more water?

Conclusions: Based on your results, which side of a leaf has more links with the air? If these links are sealed off, do you think the leaf will be less healthy? Why?

What You Need:

* A house plant, or a tree outside with branches you can reach
* Petroleum jelly
* Clear plastic wrap or plastic bags
* String or clothes pins

WHAT HAPPENS TO LEAVES WHEN LIGHT CAN'T REACH THEM?

Leaves depend on sunlight. How do you think lack of light will affect them? Decide what you think. Then do this experiment to find out.

What You Need:
* A house plant, or a tree outside with branches you can reach
* Black plastic
* Clear plastic
* String or clothespins

What to Do:

1. Fasten black plastic around a group of leaves, using string or a clothespin. Punch small holes in the plastic, so that air can reach the leaves.
2. Fasten clear plastic around another group of leaves nearby. Punch small holes as in step 1. These leaves will have the same conditions as the first group, but they'll receive light.
3. In a couple of weeks, check the leaves inside the plastic. Note their appearance. Then put the plastic back. Check again in a week or so.

Results: Did the leaves under black plastic change? Compare them to the leaves that were under clear plastic. Note any differences.

Conclusions: What did lack of light do to the leaves? How would it affect the health of the plant?

WHAT CONDITIONS HELP LEAVES DECAY?

Trees depend on nutrients in the soil. But they give back what they take. Fallen leaves decay, or break down, enriching the soil. What conditions are best for leaf decay? Do leaves decay faster when they are damp or dry, in sand or soil? Decide which conditions you think are important, and then do this experiment.

What to Do:

1. Set up your four containers. In one, bury leaves about 1 inch (2.5 cm) deep in moist soil. In another, bury leaves 1 (2.5 cm) inch deep in dry soil. In the third, bury leaves at the same depth in moist sand. In the fourth, place leaves on top of moist soil. Use the same number of leaves in each.

2. Make sure the containers with moist soil and sand are equally damp, but not soggy. Put all four containers in a dark place.

3. Check the leaves every few weeks. Note what you see.

Results: Which leaves decayed fastest?

Conclusions: Based on your results, what conditions speed leaf decay?

MORE ACTIVITIES WITH TREES AND LEAVES

1. What trees grow near your home? Take a nature walk in your neighborhood or a nearby park. Bring a notebook and a pencil. List the trees you see, using a guidebook from the library to help identify them. Which kinds of trees are most common? What unusual trees did you find?

2. Estimate the height of a tree. For this, you'll need a friend, a measuring tape, and a pencil. Here's what to do:

- Measure your friend's height with the measuring tape. Then have your friend stand right next to the tree. Walk away until you can see the entire tree, all the way to the top.

- Hold the pencil out in front of you, at arm's length, and line it up with your friend. Use your thumb to mark off a section of the pencil that corresponds to your friend's height.

- Keep your thumb in place to mark the section, and measure up the tree. Count the number of sections it takes to reach the treetop.

- To find out the tree's height, multiply that number by your friend's height. For example, suppose you count 11 pencil sections, and your friend is 4 feet (1.2 m) tall. The tree is 44 feet (13.4 m) tall—11 times 4.

3. See how water travels through stems to leaves. There are several fun ways to do this.

- Trim the end of a fresh stalk of celery. Place the stalk in water that has been colored deep red with food coloring. Put the container in bright light, and check it every few hours.

- Use two stalks of celery and two containers. Instead of colored water, put salt water in one container and sugar water in the other. Leave a stalk of celery in each container for 24 hours. Then taste the stalks.

- You may have seen green carnations on St. Patrick's Day. The carnations are colored the same way as the celery stalk. To do this, start with a white carnation. Trim the stem and put it in a strong food-coloring solution. Or make a two-tone flower—have an adult split the stem lengthwise, and put each half in a different color.

RESULTS AND CONCLUSIONS

Here are some possible results and conclusions for the activities on pages 39 to 42. Many factors may affect the results of these activities. If your results differ, try to think of reasons why. Repeat the activity with different conditions, and see if your results change.

How do leaves use water?

Leaves take in water to carry on photosynthesis, the process by which they make food. The more leaves, the more water is used. Extra water is given off through the surface of the leaf. You can see that water collecting in the plastic around the twigs.

What happens when air can't reach leaf surfaces?

You'll probably find that less water collects in the plastic when the undersides of the leaves are coated. Leaves give off water and exchange carbon dioxide and oxygen through tiny openings called stomata. Most of them are located on the underside of the leaf.

What happens to leaves when light can't reach them?

The leaves under black plastic will look pale and unhealthy. The longer they go without light, the sicklier they'll appear. They lose their chlorophyll—the substance that makes them green and allows them to capture the energy of sunlight.

What conditions help leaves decay?

Leaves buried in moist soil generally decay quickly. That's because moist soil is full of microscopic bacteria and fungi that break down dead leaves.

SOME WORDS ABOUT TREES AND LEAVES

Annual rings Bands in a cross-section of a tree trunk. They show the tree's age.

Cellulose A substance that makes up the cell walls of plants. Wood is mostly cellulose.

Chlorophyll A green pigment that allows plants to capture the energy in sunlight.

Conifers Trees that bear seeds in cones.

Deciduous With leaves that are shed in winter.

Evergreen With leaves that are kept all year.

Glucose A type of sugar produced in photosynthesis.

Photosynthesis The process by which plants use the energy in sunlight to make food.

Pigment A chemical substance that produces color.

Sap A liquid that flows through trees, carrying nutrients.

Sapling A young tree with a trunk less than 4 inches (10 cm) in diameter.

Seedling A young plant that has sprouted from seed.

Stomata (singular: stoma): Tiny openings through which leaves "breathe" and give off water.

Taproot A thick, central root that grows straight down.

FOR MORE INFORMATION

Books

Burnie, David. *Eyewitness: Tree.* New York, NY: Dorling Kindersley, 2000.

Burns, Diane L. *Trees, Leaves, and Bark* (Take-Along Guide). Thomaston, ME: Northwood Press, 1998.

Cassie, Brian, and Marjorie Burns. *Trees* (National Audubon Society First Field Guide). New York, NY: Scholastic, 1999.

Martin, Patricia Fink. *Woods and Forests.* Danbury, CT: Franklin Watts, 2000.

Robbins, Ken. *Autumn Leaves.* New York, NY: Scholastic, 1998.

Web site

American Forests

This site has information on big trees, famous and historic trees, the role of trees in the environment, and more—**http://www.americanforests.org**

INDEX

Note: Page numbers in italics indicate pictures.